Finding Your Treasure

On the Way to Healing and Hope

By

Verna G. Smith

© 2004 by Verna G. Smith. All rights reserved.

No part of this book may be reproduced, stored in a retrieval system, or transmitted by any means, electronic, mechanical, photocopying, recording, or otherwise, without written permission from the author.

ISBN: 1-4140-5913-2 (e-book)
ISBN: 1-4140-5914-0 (Paperback)

This book is printed on acid free paper.

Scripture quotations are printed in italics, and except where otherwise noted, are from the New Revised Standard Version of the Bible. Copyright © 1989 by the Division of Christian Education of the National Council of Churches of Christ in the U.S.A. and are used by permission.

Scripture labeled "THE MESSAGE" is taken from THE MESSAGE. Copyright © by Eugene H. Peterson 1993, 1994, 1995. Used by Permission of Nav Press Publishing Group.

RSV stands for Revised Standard Version, Copyright © 1946 and 1952 by the Division of Christian Education of the National Council of Churches of Christ in the U.S.A.

KJV stands for King James Version, Copyright © 1978 by Thomas Nelson, Inc.

NKJV stands for New King James Version, Copyright © 1982 by Thomas Nelson, Inc.

One quotation is from The Living Bible, Copyright © 1971 by Tyndale House Publishers, Wheaton, Illinois 60187

1stBooks - rev. 02/03/04

TABLE OF CONTENTS

INTRODUCTION v

DAY 1 OFFER GOD THE TREASURE WITHIN YOU 1

DAY 2 LET GOD'S POWER CONQUER YOUR FEARS 3

DAY 3 USE GOD'S GIFTS BOLDLY... 5

DAY 4 VALUE THE TREASURES OF DARKNESS 7

DAY 5 CLAIM THE TREASURES OF LIGHT 9

DAY 6 CHERISH THE WEALTH OF GRACE 11

DAY 7 FIND TREASURE IN YOUR DESERT 13

DAY 8 SEARCH FOR RICHES OF STILLNESS 15

DAY 9 ACCEPT GOD'S HOSPITALITY....................................... 17

DAY 10 PRACTICE HOSPITALITY TO GOD 19

DAY 11 BE HOSPITABLE TO A GRATEFUL HEART................ 21

DAY 12 MAKE YOURSELF A RESPECTED GUEST 23

DAY 13 MINE THE GOLD IN SELF LOVE 25

DAY 14 PRACTICE HOSPITALITY TO OTHERS 27

DAY 15 PRACTICE HOSPITALITY TO THOSE IN NEED 29

DAY 16 EXPLORE THE WEALTH OF LISTENING 31

DAY 17 RECOGNIZE GOD'S VISITATION................................. 33

DAY 18 TRUST THIS MINUTE.. 35

DAY 19 OPEN YOURSELF TO THE UNEXPECTED 37
DAY 20 PRACTICE HOSPITALITY TO PAIN 39
DAY 21 EMBRACE YOUR BROKENNESS 41
DAY 22 BE HOSPITABLE TO HEALING 43
DAY 23 LEARN TO LOVE YOUR LIFE 45
DAY 24 LOOK FOR GOD'S PRESENCE EVERYWHERE 47
DAY 25 WEAR THE CROWN JEWELS OF YOUR ROYALTY .. 49
DAY 26 LIVE IN GOD'S FREEDOM 51
DAY 27 SHED OUTMODED SKINS 53
DAY 28 LET LOVE TRANSCEND YOUR BOUNDARIES 55
DAY 29 LOVE YOUR GIVER MORE THAN YOUR GIFTS 57
DAY 30 TRUST GOD FOR THE HARVEST TREASURE TO COME 59
DAY 31 SEARCH FOR THE TREASURE OF DISCERNMENT .. 61
DAY 32 LISTEN FOR THE ANGELS 63
DAY 33 REBUKE THE DEMONS OF YOUR LIFE 65
DAY 34 ASK FOR DELIVERANCE FROM EVIL 67
DAY 35 COME HOME TO YOURSELF 69
DAY 36 SEEK OPPORTUNITIES IN DIMINISHMENTS 71
DAY 37 DISCOVER GOD'S PURPOSE FOR YOU. 73
DAY 38 FIND WHERE YOU BELONG. 75
DAY 39 LIVE WITH EQUILIBRIUM 77
DAY 40 LIVE VICTORIOUSLY 79

INTRODUCTION

The kingdom of heaven is like treasure hidden in a field,
which someone found and hid;
then in his joy he goes and sells all that he has
and buys that field.

Again the kingdom of heaven is like a merchant in search of fine pearls;
on finding one pearl of great value,
he went and sold all that he had
and bought it.
Matthew 13: 44-46

I want their hearts to be encouraged
and united in love,
so that they may have
all the riches of assured understanding
and have the knowledge of God's mystery,
that is, Christ himself,
in whom are hidden
all the treasures
of wisdom and knowledge.
Colossians 2: 2-3

As we discover our treasure and retain it,
we offer hospitality to God, ourselves and others.
The work of hospitality also helps us find the Treasure.

You may want to spend more than one day reflecting on each page.

Whatever you find for you
belongs to you.
Make it your own.

DAY 1 OFFER GOD THE TREASURE WITHIN YOU

Read Matthew 2:1-15

> *... opening their treasure chests, they offered him gifts of gold, frankincense, and myrrh. Matthew 2:11*

The wise men were rich people. Without material wealth, they couldn't have taken a long journey, with caravan and coterie. They had a chest of resources and knew when to use them. Their gifts later supported the infant Jesus and his family, during their exile in Egypt.

They had good minds and were people of learning. They knew the star was important, and they followed it.

They were intuitive people. They paid attention to their dreams, and therefore saved Jesus from slaughter by Herod.

Joseph, also, listened to his dream and saved his son, Jesus. He took Jesus and Mary to Egypt, where they would be safe.

We see several sources of treasure at work in this story: The wise men with their material possessions, their desire to find the Christ, and their dream; Joseph, with his caring and his dream.

Later, in Jesus' life, wealthy people supported him in his work.

> *The twelve were with him, as well as some women ... Joanna, the wife of Herod's steward, Chuza, and Susanna, and many others, who provided for them out of their resources. Luke 8:1-3*

God, who is the source of all riches, fills our lives with treasure. God can use anything we have been given, provided we commit it to God.

Verna G. Smith

When we discover our resources, we find treasure. When we learn to use our treasure, we enrich our own lives, and the lives of those around us.

PRAYER: For whatever treasure I have, our enriching God, I thank you, and I commit it to you. I trust you for discernment to use it wisely. I trust you to help me discover other resources. Thank you, my greatest treasure.

DAY 2 LET GOD'S POWER CONQUER YOUR FEARS

READ: Matthew 7:7-11

"Ask, and it will be given you; search, and you will find; knock, and the door will be opened for you."
Matthew 7:7

We may feel that we have little or nothing to offer God; we are not rich like the Wise Men; have very limited resources and few, if any gifts. We protest, "But I am poor in every way: not only financially, but in expectations, even in dreams."

At the least, we can talk with God about how we feel. Jesus taught us to go ahead and ask for our heart's desire.

We may lack power to take initiative, perhaps because of fear or depletion. I remember a bright ninth grade boy who wanted me, as the school nurse, to send him home because he felt sick. I could not find anything physically wrong, but he was scheduled to give an oral report next hour. He had prepared for it, but he was frightened. I told him I could send him home, but his next oral report would be even more difficult. I suggested another option—go back to class, and "die trying." He decided to try, and the report went very well. He needed to face his fear. Fifty percent of our battle may be a matter of showing up.

When facing difficulty, we may be tempted to say, "here goes nothing." We feel inadequate. At such a time, try saying, "here goes the power of the Creator of the universe, and that power is going with me."

Verna G. Smith

> *But we have this treasure in clay jars, so that it may be made clear that this extraordinary power belongs to God and does not come from us.*
> *2 Corinthians 4:7*

If we are depleted, we may need to rest in God, until God renews us.

PRAYER: My God of immeasurable riches, I place myself in your care, though I feel very poor. I rest in you and wait for your renewal. I thank you for whatever task you have given me this day, whether to work or to rest. I give you special thanks for your presence and power. Amen.

Finding Your Treasure

DAY 3 USE GOD'S GIFTS BOLDLY

READ: Matthew 25:14-29

> *"... the one who had received the one talent went off and dug a hole in the ground and hid his master's money. ..." Matthew 25:18*

God calls us, not to hide our gifts, but to invest them. We invest God's gifts by valuing and using them. As we use the gifts, we trust God to increase them.

The slave in our story was afraid of the owner who entrusted the talent to him. When we set aside our fears, and praise God, we increase our knowledge of God, and of ourselves. Our ability to praise God is a gift in itself.

The timid servant did not gladly receive his gift. Perhaps he compared his talent with the many talents of the other slaves. He may then have considered his lesser gift not worth caring for. It's easy to place more value on what others have, and neglect one's own potential. He rid himself of it quickly by hiding it.

> Like a child playing
> hide-and-seek
> if we hide ourselves too well
> we cannot be found

The timid child grew up with false modesty. Family and friends did not acknowledge or help him identify his gifts. They feared he would become conceited. We too, may have been fearful of acknowledging our gifts, considering them of no value. We have permitted wrong thinking to defeat us.

Verna G. Smith

We can reverse wrong thinking, by asking God's help. Then we can thoughtfully respond to invitations to serve. We may find that God is asking us to volunteer, when we perceive a need.

> *What do you have that you did not receive?*
> 1 Corinthians 4:7
>
> *What shall I return to the Lord for all his bounty to me? Psalm 116:12*

PRAYER: Our giving God, who gave the gift of your Son for us all, thank you for that most precious gift. I have not earned it. I can only receive. Thank you, also, for other gifts you have given me. Help me recognize them, value them and use them boldly. Praise you, my God.

DAY 4 VALUE THE TREASURES OF DARKNESS

READ Acts 9:1-19

> *Saul got up from the ground, and though his eyes were open, he could see nothing ...*   *Acts 9:8*
>
> *I will give you the treasures of darkness*
> *   and riches hidden in secret places,*
> *so that you may know that it is I, the Lord*
> *   the God of Israel, who call you by your name.*
> **Isaiah 45:3**

We do not like the pain of dark periods in our lives. When we become sick, or suffer loss, or failure, we sometimes feel shame, even stigma. We try most anything to remove the pain or shame. If we panic, we sometimes make the worst of all possible choices, becoming self-defeating. Periods of darkness, therefore, carry a risk. But God has promised to give us treasures during those dark times. And we can invite God to share our pain with us. "... *even the darkness is not dark to you ...*" Psalm 139:12

> *I had fainted, unless I had believed to see the goodness*
> *of the Lord in the land of the living. Wait on the Lord:*
> *be of good courage, and he shall strengthen thine*
> *heart; wait, I say, on the Lord. Psalm 27:13-14 KJV*

If we experience a loss, our periods of darkness may provide a cushion between what has been and what shall become. It is hard for us to make abrupt transitions. Even the Apostle Paul, after God called him, lived with darkness for awhile. Then he was ready to live his new life. Someone has said, "Never doubt in the dark what God has revealed in the light."

Verna G. Smith

> We do not look for darkness.
> As children we fear what
> might be there, unseen.
> As adults we fear our failures
> and other disappointments
> We lack patience. But
> our dark night helps us see the stars
> and remember them
> when dawn returns.

Our times of darkness may also give us rest. The rest will help us gather strength for our ongoing journey. And we can affirm God's promise to give us treasure in darkness.

PRAYER: God of hidden riches, I thank you for giving treasures even during my dark times, and especially then. I hold you to your promise to show me riches hidden in secret places. I believe that I shall see your goodness. Help my unbelief.

Finding Your Treasure

DAY 5 CLAIM THE TREASURES OF LIGHT

READ: John 8:12 and John 1:1-5

> *... Jesus spoke to them, saying, "I am the light of the world. Whoever follows me will never walk in darkness but will have the light of life." John 8:12*

When we are in the dark we long for the light. Fortunately, God does not intend for us to be in darkness indefinitely. He gives us a light to follow. Jesus Christ is that light. He calls us to follow him, and if we do, he promises that we will not walk in darkness.

In **Pilgrim's Progress**, Christian was not given a map for his journey. He was directed to keep his eye on the light, until he reached the gate for instructions. When we are in the dark, we wait expectantly for the Light of the World and keep our eyes fixed on him.

If we expect the light, we are attentive, and ready to receive it. Hold the thought within you, "Jesus is the light of the world." Keep thinking about the light, as you desire it for yourself.

Remember that God's light is guaranteed by God's promises. We find the promises in the Word, particularly in the Gospels and the Psalms. Affirm them at times set aside for prayer, and while working at routine tasks. Such affirmations will bring inner peace.

> *In the beginning was the Word . ... What has come into being in him was life, and the life was the light of all people. The light shines in the darkness, and the darkness did not over come it. John 1:1, 3-5*

The Quakers refer to an "inner light," not dependent upon outer circumstances.

Verna G. Smith

We can help bring God's light into our lives, and into the lives of others, through prayers of visualization. We visualize God's light within us, around us, or around someone else. Many of us are not accustomed to this kind of praying. Try it. It can be a new and rewarding experience.

PRAYER: My God of light, who sent your Son as light for the world, thank you that no darkness can overcome it. Help me to be attentive and receptive to your light. Help me to claim your promises as I live with you, Light of the World.

Finding Your Treasure

DAY 6 CHERISH THE WEALTH OF GRACE

READ: Ephesians 2:1-10

> *... by grace you have been saved, through faith, and this is not your own doing; it is the gift of God ...* **Ephesians 2:8**

> "By your death our sins are dead
> By your grace, our souls are fed."[i]

Grace is acceptance and approval that we have not earned; unmerited favor that we do not deserve. Decades of children watched *Mr Roger's Neighborhood*. They loved the late Mr. Rogers, who told them on every TV program, "I like you just the way you are." God also loves us just the way we are. When we have to take consequences for wrongdoing, our loving God stays with us, and assists us in what we are becoming. God requires only that we desire God's grace.

This grace mystifies those of us who have become accustomed to earning approval from superiors and peers. We marvel that God accepts us when we have little acceptance for ourselves.

> I sometimes yearn for strange
> things, valued in our world
> for status and for power
> But how much status do I need
> when I find my God
> and what capacity for grace
> will take me there?

PRAYER: Our accepting God, I thank you for your wonderful grace, even though I do not understand it. Sometimes, I find it hard to believe you love me just the way I am. Thank you for assisting me in what I am becoming. Thank you, my God of Grace.

Verna G. Smith

DAY 7 FIND TREASURE IN YOUR DESERT

READ: Isaiah 35:1-7

> *The wilderness and the dry land shall be glad,*
> *the desert shall rejoice and blossom;*
> *like the crocus it shall blossom abundantly,*
> *and rejoice with joy and singing ...*
> Isaiah 35:1-2

At times of loneliness or loss, our lives may feel dry as a desert. We may believe that God has deprived us, even cheated us. We fear offending God if we express our anger. We may not know that our loving God can handle our anger without retaliation. God will surprise us when we confide matters of our heart, good or bad. Our channels of communication will open, and we will be able to listen.

> *You're blessed when you're at the end of your rope.*
> *With less of you there is more of God and his rule.*
> *Matthew 5:3 THE MESSAGE*

In our desert places, God will bring unknown treasures to life within us. Wild flower seeds, in the Anza-Borrego desert in California, can lie dormant for as long as twenty years. When winter rains and other conditions are right, the desert blooms profusely, enriching countless lives.

PRAYER: God of my desert place, thank you for allowing me to speak what is in my heart. (Name those things, previously unsaid, if any.)

Thank you for preparing the right conditions for my life to blossom. I trust you for all the possibilities within me, that I did not know or even expect.

Verna G. Smith

Finding Your Treasure

DAY 8 SEARCH FOR RICHES OF STILLNESS

READ: Mark 4: 35-40

> *He ... rebuked the wind, and said to the sea, "Peace! Be still!" ... He said to them, "Why are you afraid? Have you still no faith?" Mark 4:40*

When Jesus slept during a violent storm, his terrified disciples did what you or I would do. They woke him up. First, he quieted the wind and sea, and then he spoke to their inner tumult, "Why are you afraid?" He understood the outward threat, but he was also concerned about their response.

The Psalmist also understood our inner life. After describing some of life's storms: earthquakes, war, etc., he affirms that through it all God is with us. *"Be still and know that I am God."* (Psalm 46:10)

When you are angry, disappointed, or anxious, remember:

> If Jesus stills a storm at sea,
> can He not calm a storm in me?
> Be still, my soul.

When our inner storms are raging, we are not as likely to hear Christ's voice. At such times, except in an emergency, we need to be cautious about making decisions, or taking action. After the storm subsides, we are able to listen and discern God's will.

> *Jesus, Son of David, have mercy on me! Mark 10:47*

The ancient Jesus Prayer helps us to become calm and attentive. It helps us affirm God's presence. It is most effective when we sit or lie quietly, breathe deeply, and repeat slowly for several minutes,

Verna G. Smith

> "Lord Jesus Christ
> have mercy on me."

Prayer: My quieting God, help me become inwardly still. Then, open the ears of my mind that I might hear your voice.

Lord Jesus Christ, have mercy on me. (Repeat)

DAY 9 ACCEPT GOD'S HOSPITALITY

READ: Luke 15:11-32

> *"I will get up and go to my father, and I will say to him, 'Father, I have sinned against heaven and before you; I am no longer worthy to be called your son; treat me as one of your hired hands.'" So he set off and went to his father. But while he was still far off, his father saw him and was filled with compassion; he ran and put his arms around him and kissed him. ... Luke 15:18-20*

The son who came to himself, and returned to his father, was astounded. He had not expected special privilege for he was painfully aware of his sin. He returned to confess it and ask for a job. His father received him, not as a hired servant, but as a beloved son. Then, it was up to the son to accept such undeserved hospitality.

By contrast, the older brother responded with jealous anger to his father's forgiveness of his younger brother. He was unable to enjoy the constant hospitality of his father who assured him that *"you are always with me and all that is mine is yours."* Instead, he isolated himself from his father and brother by refusing to go into the party.

> *Wrath is cruel. Anger is overwhelming. But who is able to stand before jealousy?*
> *Proverbs 27:4*

We are better able to receive God's hospitality, after we have claimed God's forgiveness. That is not to say that we should go out and commit the sins of the younger brother, in order to find forgiveness. But the older brother had no awareness of his own sins of pride and hatred, from which he needed cleansing. We may experience difficulty accepting God's hospitality, if we have not yet recognized our own sin, and asked God's forgiveness.

Verna G. Smith

Accepting forgiveness increases trust, which blossoms into thanksgiving. Trust helps us to become more hospitable to God.

PRAYER: Thank you, my hospitable God, for forgiving me when I have sinned against you. Thank you for welcoming me back, if I have strayed. Thank you that you are always with me, and all that is yours, is mine. Amen

DAY 10 PRACTICE HOSPITALITY TO GOD

READ: Psalm 92

> *It is good to give thanks to the Lord,*
> *   to sing praises to your name, O Most High;*
> *to declare your steadfast love in the morning,*
> *   and your faithfulness by night ... Psalm 92:1-2*
>
> *...the Lord takes pleasure in those who fear (revere) him,*
> *   in those who hope in his steadfast love.*
> **Psalm 147:11**

I will rejoice and be glad in my Maker this day, for the Lord takes pleasure in me.

Practicing hospitality to God sounds simple, but it may be difficult, at least initially. If so, how do we do it? I invite you to share one way that I have discovered.

> Take two index cards. On one card, write,
> It is good to declare your steadfast love in the morning.

Place it on your bedside table, or near where you sleep. In the early morning, upon awakening, even before getting out of bed, reflect on the words. Let them stay with you, as you rise to begin your day.

> On the other card, write,
> It is good to declare your faithfulness by night.

Place it also near your bed and reflect on those words just before going to sleep. Thank your God who is faithful, watching over you and protecting you from undesirable forces, even while you sleep.

Verna G. Smith

>PRAYER: Praise you, my God, who loves me
>Praise you, my God, who stays with me
>persistently
>like the shining sun behind the clouds
>when I don't know it's there.
>Praise you, my God.

Finding Your Treasure

DAY 11 BE HOSPITABLE TO A GRATEFUL HEART

READ: Exodus 17:1-7

> *... the people there thirsted for water; and the people complained against Moses, and said, "Why did you bring us out of Egypt, to kill us and our children and livestock with thirst?" Exodus 17:3*

As they wandered in the desert, the Israelites kept complaining. They were so stuck in their complaints that they even wanted to run back to an impossible former life. Moses took the grumbling to God, asking, "What shall I do?"

Complaints may be valid. It's important to be aware of them, and to know the right time and place to express them. They may give us a clue about our next step in life. And we can ask God how to act on our complaints.

We also need to pay attention to our complaints for another reason. They may prevent us from listening to God. At such a time, we can help ourselves by asking, "What is God saying to me in this place, in this situation?" If we still don't know what to do, we can start by thanking God for God's help which is already on the way. God will tell us how God wants to use us.

> *Those who bring thanksgiving as their sacrifice, honor me. Psalm 50: 23*

Verna G. Smith

> How easy and
> how wide the road
> for complaints.
> How narrow and
> precipitous
> the road of gratitude.
> Gratitude requires effort
> an uphill climb
> and it renews,
> separating
> wheat from chaff
> in our lives,
> and opens us to God.

PRAYER: Thank you, God of the past and the future, who even now works on behalf of each one of us. I trust you to show me the way, as you lead in the way everlasting.

DAY 12 MAKE YOURSELF A RESPECTED GUEST

READ: MARK 6:1-6

> *"Where did this man get all this? ... Is not this the carpenter, the son of Mary and brother of James and Joses and Judas and Simon, and are not his sisters with us?" ... And he could do no deed of power there, except that he laid his hands on a few sick people and cured them. And he was amazed at their unbelief. Mark 6:2-3, 5-6*

When I worked with juvenile offenders, we were careful to treat them with respect, in order to help them respect themselves. Initially, it was not easy to show respect to people skilled in taking advantage of perceived "softness." But we combined respect with a demanding toughness. We taught them to respect themselves, their clothes, property, and other people. They needed self-respect to recover from a depressive life style. Previously, they had been governed only by their impulse of the moment, which led them into serious trouble.

As we read the story of Jesus' return to his hometown, we learn how little the people of Nazareth respected themselves. "Who does he think he is? He's only one of us." ONE OF US! They could not believe that God could break through their ordinary lives (their own town; a carpenter; a CARPENTER!). Such a mind set prevented their taking advantage of a marvelous opportunity. If they had held greater self-respect, they would have been able to receive God's most precious gift for them, Jesus himself. Instead, they became hostile, and even tried to destroy him. (Luke 4:28-30)

Such lack of respect for themselves, and for him, diminished Jesus' power. This event in Nazareth is the only recorded time of diminishment during Jesus' ministry.

Verna G. Smith

PRAYER: Loving God, thank you for your respect for all your creation, including me. Teach me to respect myself and others, that I might be able to receive more of your wonderful gifts. Amen

Finding Your Treasure

DAY 13 MINE THE GOLD IN SELF LOVE

READ: Mark 12:28-31

> *"The second (commandment) is this: 'You shall love your neighbor as yourself.' ..."*
> *Mark 12:31*

We are most likely to reject hospitality to ourselves when we don't love ourselves enough. How do we learn to love ourselves?

We love ourselves when we respect ourselves, and come to know who we are. But how do you know yourself? Begin by noticing what is important to you, what makes you angry, what draws out your best. What leads you away from your best? Do you dislike anything about yourself? Do parts of your past life come to mind uninvited and unwelcome? Look at them carefully with love. Is God calling you to ask for cleansing? Is God calling you to love some part of yourself and your life that you have not loved before?

What will happen if you love all of you, without exception, as God loves you? You will begin to value yourself. You will cherish this person, made in God's image. You will give yourself the nurturing you need. You will live hospitably to yourself. This may be particularly difficult if you did not experience hospitality in early life. Were you not cared for? Did you believe you were of no worth? Such former destructive attitudes lose power when you practice hospitality to yourself. Ask God to help you when you find it difficult.

> Affirm:
> There's good stuff in me
> like gold in a mountain stream
> but it needs sifting, smelting, and refining
> and combining into beauty.

Verna G. Smith

PRAYER: My valuing God, help me care for my new life that I am becoming. I will not leave my care to happenstance, or completely to other people. I trust you to teach me how to know, and love myself. Thank you that I am your loving, precious child.

Finding Your Treasure

DAY 14 PRACTICE HOSPITALITY TO OTHERS

READ: Luke 14:15-24

> *" ... the owner of the house ... said to his slave, 'Go out at once into the streets and lanes of the town and bring in the poor, the crippled, the blind, and the lame.' ..." Luke 14:21*

Because God is hospitable, we can be hospitable, too.

- AT MY TABLE

The person God invites, I invite
The angel God invites, I invite
The life force God invites, I invite

How shall I discern God's invitation
when I live in a world with attitudes
different from God's? We look for people
who reward us with power, influence,
money, their reflected glory

How shall I notice the least of these,
unattractive, whom God invited to my
table, asking me to love and care?
How shall I know the story of the hurts
beneath the glittering person whom
I regard as superficial?
How shall I recognize the wounds of
those whose gifts elicit jealousy?
How shall I know the Christ within the
vulnerable, whom I despise or fear?

Verna G. Smith

> I can only ask for help, so that
> The person God invites, I also invite.

PRAYER: My hospitable God, whomever you have invited to my table, help me receive with your same hospitality.

DAY 15 PRACTICE HOSPITALITY TO THOSE IN NEED

READ: Matthew 25:31-40

> *"Then the king will say to those at his right hand, 'Come, you that are blessed by my Father, inherit the kingdom prepared for you ... for I was hungry and you gave me food, I was thirsty and you gave me something to drink, I was a stranger and you welcomed me, I was naked and you gave me clothing, I was sick and you took care of me, I was in prison and you visited me.' ... Truly I tell you, just as you did it to one of the least of these who are members of my family, you did it to me." Matthew 25:34-36, 40*

I will practice hospitality to needy people that God reveals, especially the very young or old, the unattractive, or the suffering. I will show kindness to those who "have everything." No one has everything. We only think they do. I will welcome strangers, remembering we are all exiles.

God has made me and fashioned me, just as God has created every person I meet today. As I meet people who love me, I will thank God for love and friendship.

If I meet someone who irritates me, I will try to know that person better. I will offer a silent prayer, thanking God for the lives of both of us. I will visualize God's light around us.

> *"Keep open house; be generous with your lives. By opening up to others, you'll prompt people to open up with God, this generous Father in heaven. ...."*
> *Matthew 5:16 THE MESSAGE*

Verna G. Smith

I will be aware that behaviors and attitudes can be caught, whether they are positive or negative. I will use the motto: "Act as if," suggested by C. S. Lewis when he wrote,

> *"Do not waste time bothering whether you 'love' your neighbor; act as if you did. As soon as we do this we find one of the great secrets. When you are behaving as if you loved someone, you will presently come to love him."*[ii]

PRAYER: My loving God, thank you for making me in your image. Thank you for calling me to love. It's hard to do, sometimes. Thank you that you are with me and are teaching me how to be hospitable to your children.

DAY 16 EXPLORE THE WEALTH OF LISTENING

READ: Mark 9:2-8

> *Peter said to Jesus, "Rabbi, it is good for us to be here; let us make three dwellings, one for you, one for Moses, and one for Elijah." He did not know what to say, for they were terrified. Mark 9:5-6*

Peter, who did not know what to say, spoke anyway. In his fear, he spoke too soon.

> *Let everyone be quick to listen, slow to speak ... James 1:19*

We know how difficult it is to be with a person in an awesome event, and listen contemplatively. Impulsively, we want to "do something," to be helpful.

Sometimes, words spoken carelessly can hurt. They may stay with us a long time, taking on a life of their own. Jesus said, ".... *The simple moral fact is that words kill ...*" (Matthew 5:22 THE MESSAGE). The old saying, "Sticks and stones will break my bones but words will never hurt me," is not always valid. A woman told me, after her husband's death, his sister said, "Bess, you will just have to take care of yourself, now." The well intentioned words spoken to a grieving widow wounded her for a long time. Again, a mother told her young child, after he stumbled on a curb, "You're always so clumsy."

Words have power to hurt, but words, rightly chosen, can comfort, encourage, and heal. Such restoring words will likely come out of contemplative listening. We ask God to help us hear with our entire selves, and respond as God prompts us. We use a love filter with what we hear, remembering that *"Just as water reflects the face, so one* human heart reflects another." (Proverbs 27:19). We put aside judging and jealousy that block our generosity and choke our energy.

> *... where there is envy and selfish ambition, there will also be disorder and wickedness of every kind.*
> *James 3:16*

Listening involves responsibility. God will teach us how to listen, and how to respond, if we ask.

PRAYER: Our ever listening God, teach me how to be present through listening. Help me use love for filtering what I hear, and reflecting another heart. Help me honor you with my thoughts before my words begin to form. Thank you, my teaching God.

DAY 17 RECOGNIZE GOD'S VISITATION

Read: Luke 19:41-44

> *As he came near and saw the city, he wept over it, saying, "If you, even you, had only recognized on this day the things that make for peace! But now they are hidden from your eyes. ... you did not recognize the time of your visitation from God." Luke 19:41, 42, 44*

If we do not recognize our visitations, we may become hostile to our experiences, or at best, ignore them. We have seen how the people of Nazareth did not understand that God was visiting them through their home town boy, Jesus. Now, in our reading, we are reflecting upon how Jesus mourns over Jerusalem, the religious center of his day. Many people, especially those in power, did not recognize their visitation. They were upset by Jesus' actions and his teaching. When we are upset by circumstances, our impulse may be to react quickly from our anger. The Psalmist speaks to this,

> *When you are disturbed, do not sin;*
> *ponder it on your beds, and be silent. Psalms 4:4*

Whatever comes, we can still find God with us. Something may have happened that isn't our fault at all. God has not wished us to suffer, and longs to comfort us in our distress.

At such times, we may be able to recognize God's visitation, as did an American friend, who was imprisoned by the Japanese in the Philippines, during World War II. Every morning, upon awakening, she pondered, "What does God want me to learn from this day?" She discovered that she was called to receive grace.

If you are troubled by traumatic experiences from your past, ask God to help you forgive and accept God's healing. God will not forsake you.

Verna G. Smith

When you experience disappointment, you may find the following prayer helpful,

> "Keep me friendly to myself,
> keep me gentle in disappointment."[iii]

PRAYER: My gracious God, when you come to me, and I do not recognize you, help my soul to be still. I trust you in every experience. Help my lack of trust.

DAY 18 TRUST THIS MINUTE

READ: I Samuel 3:1-19

> *Then Eli perceived that the Lord was calling the boy. Therefore, Eli said to Samuel, "Go, lie down; and if he calls you, you shall say, 'Speak Lord, for your servant is listening.'" 1 Samuel 3:8-9*

The boy, Samuel, did not recognize God's call, but Eli did. With Eli's instruction, Samuel opened himself to God, and invited the Lord to speak.

We too, may receive a call in the night when we waken, unable to sleep. We can trust God for the sleeplessness, and be attentive to what is happening. Is God ready to tell us something that we are better able to hear in the stillness of the night? We can open ourselves to God by thanking God for His presence, and asking God to help us receive his message. The Lord may have something for us to do. Perhaps God wants us to be aware of a need we have, or that someone else has. God will reveal. Trust the moment, and then follow through, at the right time.

During the day, some of us are too busy thinking about what comes next. We hurry, wanting to get on with more important things. With my busyness, I am likely to become irritated while standing in line at the deli or supermarket. Then I can begin to remember God's presence in this moment, which otherwise may seem insignificant..

> *"Whoever is faithful in a very little is faithful also in much ..." Luke 16:10*

It's helpful to try living each day as if it were the last day of our lives, as taught by Anthony of Egypt, in the fourth century.

Verna G. Smith

PRAYER: Thank you, my trustworthy God, for every moment of my waking or sleeping life. Thank you that you are with me every minute; that time with you is never wasted. Thank you for helping me be attentive to your Spirit right now. Amen.

DAY 19 OPEN YOURSELF TO THE UNEXPECTED

READ: Matthew 2:23-15

... an angel of the Lord appeared to Joseph in a dream and said, "Get up, take the child and his mother, and flee to Egypt ..." Matthew 2:13

When Joseph was warned in a dream not to return home with Mary and his infant son, his family suddenly had to make other plans. They traveled to Egypt, to join a Jewish community living in exile.

Most of us, like Joseph, have lived with sudden changes from shattered expectations. Recently, I have looked back on my high school years, when I had to work for my room and board, instead of living at home with my own family. Remembering, I became sad; not because of the circumstances that made me homeless, but because I was unable to do gladly what I needed to do. I could have made it easier for myself and my mother.

Fifth century monks, living in the desert, understood the flexibility needed for living graciously. They admonished each other to fast before the Lord, according to their strength. They used fasting with prayer as preparation for God's presence. And though individual fasting was very important to them, they also taught, "If there is a meeting of the brethren, and you have to eat a second or third time, do not be disgruntled and surly. On the contrary, do gladly what you have to do, and when you have eaten a second or a third time, thank God that you have fulfilled the law of love and that He himself is providing for you."[iv]

We may have our own agenda for this day, or even this week or this year. And suddenly, it must shift. We can ask God to help us remain at peace with the change. Our peace will free us from worry about

Verna G. Smith

what we had desired or planned. It will also help prevent our frantically hurrying and making mistakes, even in small things.

> *Rejoice in the Lord always; again, I will say, Rejoice.*
> *Philippians 4:4*

>> Do gladly what you have to do.
>> When you're at a party, or even at church
>> and meeting or welcoming a stranger
>> when you would rather stay with old friends.

PRAYER: Our God of peace, thank you for giving us peace when we experience some of life's unwelcome events.

(Name them, if there are any.)

Help me to do gladly what I am called upon to do, even though I don't feel glad about it. I trust you to help me live out the law of love.

Finding Your Treasure

DAY 20 PRACTICE HOSPITALITY TO PAIN

READ: Philippians 4:4-14

> *Don't fret or worry. Instead of worrying, pray. Let petitions and praises shape your worries into prayers, letting God know your concerns. Before you know it, a sense of God's wholeness, everything coming together for good, will come and settle you down. It's wonderful what happens when Christ displaces worry at the center of your life.*
> *Philippians 4:6-7 THE MESSAGE*

Practice hospitality to pain at least long enough to know what to do with it. We may have experienced one of life's greatest disappointments: the death of a spouse, a parent, a child, or even a close friend. Rejection by a spouse, or loss of a cherished position can bring intense pain. So can the memory of losing parental love as a child. And pain may come from many other sources, including disease or physical injury. It can be excruciating, or just annoying.

God calls us to resist becoming intimidated by our own pain, or by the pain of others. We tend to fear it, and want to run away or ignore it. As parents, we want to spare our children.

We don't look for suffering. But sometimes pain calls our attention to something in our lives that needs correction. It may serve as a vehicle to help us move from one place in our lives to another. It also may accompany healing processes. God is the healer of pain.

When pain strikes that has no useful purpose, other than catching our attention, we may need medical assistance to control it. Remember that God stays with us in our pain. We can converse with God about it, for God longs to comfort us and set us free. God does not intend for any of us to suffer pain indefinitely.

Verna G. Smith

PRAYER: My delivering God, I place myself in your tender mercy and your care. I entrust you with all the experiences of life, even its greatest pain. Especially,

> I thank you for the pain of healing
> I thank you for the healing of pain.

I trust you. Help my lack of trust.

Finding Your Treasure

DAY 21 EMBRACE YOUR BROKENNESS

READ: Luke 22:17-20

> *Then he took a loaf of bread, and when he had given thanks, he broke it and gave it to them, saying, "This is my body, which is given for you. Do this in remembrance of me." Luke 22:19*

I once heard Henri Nouwen speak of embracing our brokenness as Christ embraced his broken body. Our brokenness includes anything in our past or present, which we feel stigmatizes or shames us.

Sometimes we take an impossible burden upon ourselves. We believe that God accepts nothing less than perfection. We become afraid of the messes in our lives. God sees our imperfections differently. God sees what we are becoming.

Sometimes we easily embrace our brokenness, and gain instant relief from our burdens. Other times, we encounter our own resistance.

> I want to embrace
> my brokenness
> and be healed, but
> brokenness is full
> of thorns, sharp
> and piercing, and I
> wonder what to do.
>
> I'll soak the thorns in
> waters of my grief, and
> soften them until they
> bend upon themselves
> and then I shall embrace
> my brokenness.

Verna G. Smith

The ultimate brokenness in our lives is our impending death. The playwright, Saroyan, is reputed to have said, "I know everybody dies, but I thought when they came to me, they'd make an exception." In contrast, Anthony of Egypt perceived death as a fulfillment of a life lived with God.

PRAYER: Merciful God, have mercy on me. Help me embrace my broken life until it becomes whole, compassionate and free.

DAY 22 BE HOSPITABLE TO HEALING

READ: Mark 5: 24-34

> *Immediately her hemorrhage stopped; and she felt in her body that she was healed of her disease. Immediately aware that power had gone forth from him, Jesus turned about in the crowd and said, "Who touched my clothes?"*
> *Mark 5:29-30*

Jesus wanted to say something further to this desperate woman who had received such a dramatic cure. He wanted her to understand her part in the healing. She had been audacious, certain that touching his garment would be enough. Jesus gave validity to her feelings. How different from the experiences of some of us, when friends have described our healing as "coincidental." Jesus, also, wanted her to be at peace with her ongoing life. It would be very different, now. He knew that any change, including an improved life, can sometimes bring anxiety.

> I called you because
> I want to know more about
> you and your healing.
> I want to know the
> longings of your heart
> and how I touched you
> when you touched me.
>
> But it's not all up to me.
> Your faith became the
> bond between us, that
> has made you well. Give
> up your fear; your weeping
> and your trembling, and
> take my peace instead.

Verna G. Smith

As we ponder this event, we are likely to focus on the healed woman, and to miss Jesus' personal experience. He was *"immediately aware that power had gone forth from him."* He gave up energy from within himself.

God may call us, not only to receive healing, but also to convey God's healing. If so, we may give up energy, even though God does the work. We then quietly wait upon God to renew us. We pray for protection, that we do not absorb any evil that has been released in the process.

PRAYER: My healing God, thank you for healing my life. Thank you for releasing anxiety that might accompany it. And when you call me as instrument of healing for someone else, help me give willingly of myself. Protect me and renew me. Amen

DAY 23 LEARN TO LOVE YOUR LIFE

READ: Isaiah 45:9-12

> *Woe to you who strive with your Maker,*
> *earthen vessels with the potter!*
> *Does the clay say to the one who fashions it,*
> *"What are you making?"*
> *or "Your work has no handles?" Isaiah 45:9*

In the fourth century, one of our great Christian mystics, Anthony, taught that knowing and loving ourselves helps us know and love God. And knowing and loving God helps us love ourselves and other people.

> And God said, I cannot show my love for
> you completely unless you love yourself.
> You are the vehicle for my love, directed
> to you— In the past, some were channels
> and they failed. In the present, others
> are transmitting. But part of my love comes
> to you— through you.

Your hands have made and fashioned me. Psalm 119:73

> IN THE FIRING
> I want to use you, my child
> but first, prepare you:
> place you on my potter's
> wheel; center you; water you.

Verna G. Smith

> Do not be disturbed
> by your cleansing
> tears, while I spin
> and shape you,
> or afterward, when I place
> you in the fire
> and glaze, and fire
> again, before I fill
> you, my precious vessel.

PRAYER: Thank you, my Creator God. You have made me and are making me anew every day. I trust you to fill me with your love, that I might love you more deeply, and love the treasure of my life that you have given me.

DAY 24 LOOK FOR GOD'S PRESENCE EVERYWHERE

READ: Matthew 5:1-11

> *"You're blessed when you get your inside world—your mind and heart—put right. Then you can see God in the outside world. ..."*
> *Matthew 5:8, THE MESSAGE*

Look for the movement of God in every circumstance. Then ask, "Where is God in this event, and in my life?"

YOU ARE THE KING

You are the King of the universe
You created the stars, and
formed us from the same dust
as their celestial bodies.

You are the Prince of Peace
Your consolations calm our
spirits in life's raging storms

You are the Good Shepherd who
carries us when we are lost
protects us from wild beasts and
demons, subtle in destruction

You are the Healer of life's hurts
and its diseases. You take our
burdens, carry them each day

Verna G. Smith

>You are the sacrificial Lamb
>who takes away the sins of the world
>You forgive us, show your love
>by not remembering our sins
>
>You are too wonderful for me.
>I could not have imagined such a God.

PRAYER: An evening prayer for frequent use:

Make the answer to this question your prayer. What am I most grateful for this day?

Finding Your Treasure

DAY 25 WEAR THE CROWN JEWELS OF YOUR ROYALTY

READ: Romans 8:14-17

For all who are led by the Spirit of God are children of God. ... and if children, then heirs, heirs of God and joint heirs with Christ ... Romans 8:14, 17

Sing praises to God, sing praises;
  sing praises to our King, sing praises.
For God is the king of all the earth;
  sing praises with a Psalm. Psalm 47:6-7

Since God the Father is the King, we are sons and daughters of the King. God will reveal to you what your royalty means.

I am a daughter of the King
I'm regal, but not overbearing
I am a daughter of the King
I'm elegant, but not superior
I am a daughter of the King
gracious and compassionate
but no patsy

I am a daughter of the King
I'm clothed in my right mind
of finest purple, unconcerned
about appearances. I have my
friends, but I am lonely, too

I am a daughter of the King
I will discern
and judgments won't be harsh

Verna G. Smith

PRAYER: I praise you, my Father King, for making me your beloved son/daughter.

Finding Your Treasure

DAY 26 LIVE IN GOD'S FREEDOM

READ: Acts 12: 6-11

> *... Peter, bound with two chains, was sleeping between two soldiers, while guards in front of the door were keeping watch over the prison. Suddenly an angel of the Lord appeared ... the chains fell off his wrist. ... Peter went out and followed him; ... they came before the iron gate leading into the city. It opened for them of its own accord, and they went outside ... Peter came to himself and said, "Now I am sure that the Lord has sent his angel and rescued me ..." Acts 12:6-11*

I remember how we farm children were taught to lock the barn door after we led horses out of a burning barn. Otherwise, the horses would run back inside. When God sets us free from prison by loosening our chains, God invites us to walk away. When Peter's chains fell off, God's messenger was there to lead him out. And, at times, God may send messengers to lead us out of our prisons.

God may not always lock our barn doors behind us, for instance, when we're giving up an addiction. But God gives us strength to resist returning.

We may not always experience a dramatic release. Sometimes we feel the anguish of the Psalmist who wrote, *"... no refuge remains to me; no one cares for me."* (Psalm 142: 4) After my father died, how many times did I hear my mother say, "No one cares for me!"? Some people did take advantage of her vulnerability. But many did not. I did not then understand the power of depressive forces to imprison.

Sometimes God liberates us within our prison. Nothing is changed outwardly, only our inner selves. Certain moods and other attitudes of mind become different. Paul alluded to this when he wrote, *"Even*

Verna G. Smith

though our outer nature is wasting away, our inner nature is being renewed day by day." (2 Corinthians 4:16)

> God is my freedom
> I can now discard my chains
> and walk with God
> God teaches me; I am free to learn
> God loves me; I am free to love
> God strengthens me; I am free to serve
> God gives me peace; I can live with confidence

Bring me out of prison, so that I may give thanks to your name. Psalm 142:7

PRAYER: My liberating God, I trust you to release me from whatever imprisons me. Show me the prisons I can walk away from, and show me the prisons within, where I can find deliverance. Help me welcome the freedom that you give. Thank you, my liberating God.

DAY 27 SHED OUTMODED SKINS

READ: John 11:17-44

> *... he cried with a loud voice, "Lazarus, come out." The dead man came out, his hands and feet bound with strips of cloth, and his face wrapped in a cloth. Jesus said to them, "Unbind him, and let him go."*
> *John 11:43-44*

Just as Lazarus left his grave cloths behind, we need to leave ours, like a snake shedding its skin. In ancient times, people regarded snakes as symbols of healing. They perceived transformation in the shedding of outmoded skins. When Jesus gave new life to Lazarus, bound in grave cloths, he instructed people around him to "Unbind him and let him go."

We may be in old skins that need to go. Shedding them ought not to be painful, unless we are keeping them alive by nourishing them: cherishing old grudges, or "what might have been." We can ask God whether something within us is enjoying anger, or a grudge, or self pity. Nurturing the new skin underneath, helps us shed the old.

After my father died, I lived with my maternal grandmother for a year and a half. She openly showed her resentment for caring for me, a nine year old. At the same time, I noticed she was tender and loving to my baby sister. I cannot condone her rejection, though I understand it. I found my old skin of resentment difficult to shed.

I could cast it off only through a process of forgiving her, and growing love for my own grandchildren and my sister. Friends also assisted by praying for me during my time of distress.

Verna G. Smith

> Unbind her and let her go
> you said of me
> bound in grave cloths of my past
> like Lazarus constricted.
> You gave new life, but
> many loving hands and hearts
> have helped unbind to let me go.

PRAYER: Loving Father, if I have an old skin constricting me, I offer it to you right now. (Name it) I trust you to help me understand it, and grow the new life that sheds the old. Thank you, my trustworthy God.

DAY 28 LET LOVE TRANSCEND YOUR BOUNDARIES

READ: 2 Corinthians 5:14-17

> *... the love of Christ controls us.*
> *2 Corinthians 5:14 RSV*

A boundary is that which fixes a limit. Some boundaries serve a useful purpose in our lives. They help provide power with safety. River water that is bounded and fed through an outlet can be transformed into usable energy. A hospital bed, with treatment, gives safe boundaries during critical illness. Christ's love is like that.

Other boundaries may obstruct the best in us and we need to transcend them. We may be imposing some boundaries upon ourselves. Perhaps we are unwilling to forgive ourselves for failures and sins of our past, or to claim God's forgiveness.

The love of Christ gives us power to transcend boundaries that limit our full potential or that injure and destroy. Reconciling love transforms us into new creations.

We may not love ourselves enough to accept changes in our life patterns. I have dealt with capable young children who were nevertheless failing in school. They were maintaining emotional boundaries of infancy. A twelve year old boy once told me he wished he could stay the same age and never grow older. His self-limiting desire was preventing his mastery of important developmental tasks.

We may set up boundaries for ourselves because we do not appreciate our own gifts. And we may keep boundaries in place with others because we envy them or fear them. We may impose boundaries by unrealistic expectations or over-scheduling.

Verna G. Smith

If we're hurrying like lemmings toward life's cliffs
what transformations will we miss?

If my agenda is too full, and I continue pushing
envelopes of fatigue, as I have for many years
what transformation lurks, then disappears?

If I ignore my dreams as weird
If I reject the least of these:
poor, oppressed, diseased

What transformation might have come and made a home
and opened up a life as yet unknown?

PRAYER: God of unbounded love, teach me which boundaries in my life are useful and which I can transcend with your help. Thank you, my teaching God.

Finding Your Treasure

DAY 29 LOVE YOUR GIVER MORE THAN YOUR GIFTS

READ: Luke 18:9-14

> *" ... The Pharisee, standing by himself, was praying thus, 'God, I thank you that I am not like other people ...'" Luke 18:11*

Sometimes we become so attached to our gifts that we forget where they come from. The Pharisee forgot that God had given him a good mind and helped him to gain an education and to lead a religious life. He also enjoyed a privileged status in society. Taking the attitude that he had produced his own gifts, he held the tax collector in contempt. He was really praying to himself.

We owe approval and gratitude to the one who gives the gifts, rather than to the one who receives them. As recipients, we gain approval when we receive our gifts graciously, and nurture them.

We may not recognize some of our gifts as gifts. The promises of God are gifts. Friendships are precious gifts, as are loved ones.

We need to give thanks for the gifts and blessings of our lives, being careful not to organize our lives around them. It will help if we listen for the call of God, even in the midst of our blessings.

When some of life's gifts are gone, we can remember that God's resources are inexhaustible. God will provide other gifts, if we are ready to receive them.

> *You show me the path of life.*
> *In your presence there is fullness of joy;*
> *in your right hand are pleasures forevermore.*
> *Psalm 16:11*

Verna G. Smith

PRAYER: My generous God, thank you for your wonderful gifts (name them).

Help me to keep all in perspective, and love you more than your gifts.

DAY 30 TRUST GOD FOR THE HARVEST TREASURE TO COME

READ: Matthew 13:24-30

"Let both of them (weeds and wheat) grow until the harvest" Matthew 13: 30

A common weed of Jesus' day was the poisonous bearded darnel. The young plant looked like wheat. But by the time it could be distinguished from wheat, the roots were intertwined. Pulling up the bad would also bring up the good.

Evil may have come into our lives when we were young and couldn't help it. Or even later when we had no control over events. We have given ourselves to God, but some of the effects are still present.

Our experiences in life shape and mold us. Hopefully, we have claimed forgiveness for sins we were responsible for. But how about things that happened that weren't our fault? Those events are weeds. Some of the weeds of my young life related to ostracism of my mother by some of my father's relatives, after his death. I loved all of them, but my greatest loyalty was to my mother. I was torn.

> All my experiences in life
> what are good and what are bad
> God will decide
> which were wheat, and which were weeds
> planted surreptitiously.
>
> God will not lobotomize
> my memories
> eradicating weeds
> else I, too, might be destroyed.

Verna G. Smith

>I am free, now
>from the worry and the guilt
>of my weeds
>God will wait to separate
>in order to preserve.

PRAYER: My harvesting God, thank you that the weeds in my life cannot choke the Spirit. I entrust them to your care. I thank you that you don't like them any better than I do. Thank you for the day of harvest when you will remove them permanently.

DAY 31 SEARCH FOR THE TREASURE OF DISCERNMENT

READ: Mark 3: 20-30

> *"How can Satan cast out Satan? If a kingdom is divided against itself, that kingdom cannot stand. And if a house is divided against itself, that house will not be able to stand. ..." Mark 3:23-25*

The scribes accused Jesus of casting out demons by the power of the prince of demons. Jesus spoke harshly about their lack of discernment. They attributed his manifested power of God to evil.

When we discern, we show good judgment or understanding. When we receive discernment, we understand God's desires and intentions for us. We interpret events in our lives. We know what to ask for. We know how to proceed.

God helps us discern the many voices or thoughts that want to influence us.

> Voices call for my attention
> competing vendors in my
> marketplace of inner self
> Come see this! Over here, mam!
> I have the best!
>
> I twist and turn, develop vertigo
> I cannot attend to all.
> Heaviness descends
> darkness creeps inside
> I want to please too many.

Verna G. Smith

> Can I now rely upon my inner
> light, not the same as yours?
> Maybe what is right for you
> is not right for me.

Some of the means God provides for helping us in discernment, include Scripture, our own meditation and stillness, and a trusted spiritual friend. Take care to use these generous, wonderful resources. When we discern the treasures we already have, we give thanks for them. A thankful heart maintains a hopeful heart.

PRAYER: My generous God, increase your gift which attracts me to you as God of my life. Help me discern your wonderful gifts around me and within. I thank you for them. (Name them.) Help me discern your intentions for me and for my life. Thank you, my discerning God.

DAY 32 LISTEN FOR THE ANGELS

READ: Acts 10: 1-33

> *About noon ... Peter went up on the roof to pray. He became hungry and wanted something to eat; and ... fell into a trance. He saw ... all kinds of four-footed creatures and reptiles and birds of the air. Then he heard a voice saying, "Get up, Peter; kill and eat." But Peter said, "By no means, Lord; for I have never eaten anything that is profane or unclean." ... The voice said ... "What God has made clean, you must not call profane." Acts 10:9-15*

In Biblical events, God often used dreams and visions or angels to give messages to people, or minister to them. Angels often came at periods of bodily quiet, during sleep, or while fasting. In a dream, an angel told Joseph to take Mary as his wife. (Matthew 1:20) The shepherds were keeping watch at night when angels revealed God's message concerning Jesus' birth. (Luke 2: 9-10) After Jesus fasted, and resisted evil temptation, angels ministered to him. (Matthew 4:11)

In today's scripture reading, Cornelius is described as one who "*prayed constantly to God*" Peter was at prayer, while waiting for his lunch, when he saw the heaven opened.

We learn from scriptures to value the times of forced waiting, even boredom, or sleepless periods at night. Try to be still. These may be the times that God chooses for sending messengers of light.

> *When you are disturbed, ... ponder it on your beds, and be silent. Psalms 4:4*

Be especially attentive to unexpected events, to illness or injury: anything likely to make you afraid.

Verna G. Smith

> *The angel of the Lord encamps around those who fear (revere) him, and delivers them. Psalms 34:7*

"Fear not," the angels often say in scripture. Initially, we may respond with fear. But ultimately, they bring us peace, and then freedom to take action.

PRAYER: My God of quietness, I give myself to you. I wait upon you and your messengers, to speak to me, and give your peace. And then I shall know how to proceed.

DAY 33 REBUKE THE DEMONS OF YOUR LIFE

READ: Luke 11: 24-26

> *"When the unclean spirit has gone out of a person, it wanders through waterless regions looking for a resting place, but not finding any, it says, 'I will return to my house from which I came.' When it comes, it finds it swept and put in order. Then it goes and brings seven other spirits more evil than itself, and they enter and live there; and the last state of that person is worse than the first."*
> **Luke 11:24-26**

The demons of our lives are the opposite of angels. They are any forces or impulses that would lead us away from God. They do not bring us lasting peace or joy.

In Jesus' parable the demon returns with seven other demons because it finds the house swept and empty. When God fills our lives, God protects us from evil, and gives us power to resist the dark forces that love to return to an empty house. We insure God's presence by keeping his commandments, and praying. Besides our own prayers, we need the prayers of our friends. Fasting also prepares us, if our health and circumstances permit.

When we are not aware of evil forces, we are most likely to be influenced by them. Our discerning God helps us recognize demons that trouble us. When we recognize our subtle demons, we can dismiss them. As we resist forces of darkness, we develop our ability to identify and confront them.

If demons or forces of darkness trouble you with events from your past, remember those events belonged to your pupa stage. God is making you a butterfly now. You don't see butterflies hovering around their discarded cocoon. They're flying and gathering nectar and doing what they were created to do.

After rebuking forces of darkness, ask Jesus to continue filling you with God's loving presence, which continues to protect you.

PRAYER: In the name of Jesus of Nazareth, son of Joseph and Mary, son of the living God. If any troubling forces of darkness are present, leave me now. Go directly to Jesus who will know what to do with you. Do not linger or go to anyone else.

My delivering God, free me from anything within me that connects with evil temptations. But do not leave me empty. Fill my inner self with your protection and power. Keep me in your care and mercy.

DAY 34 ASK FOR DELIVERANCE FROM EVIL

READ: Matthew 4: 1-11

> *Then Jesus was led up by the Spirit into the wilderness to be tempted by the devil.*
> *Matthew 4:1*

None of us is immune to evil temptation. Jesus, who was filled with the Holy Spirit, was tempted to doubt who he was, and what he had been called to do. He was tempted to take on status and fame, rather than the sins of the world. After he had resisted the doubts concerning his identity and purpose, he was tempted to use his powers to do something foolish: jump off a high place to test God's willingness to rescue him.

> *And do not bring us to the time of trial, but rescue us from the evil one.*
> *Matthew 6:13*

We sometimes forget the very strong caution Jesus gave us concerning evil. He instructed us to pray for deliverance. We may not recognize evil if it fits in with our circumstances. How easily the demons can speak to us through our own agenda.

They love to trouble us through wounded pride. They look for ways to hook into unresolved pain in our past; pain that is now triggered by present events or people.

Sometimes, as we walk more closely with God, we become aware of past sins that may not have been forgiven. They can torment us pitilessly until we claim God's forgiveness, and forgive ourselves. We may become painfully aware of our failures.

Verna G. Smith

> So take away the sting of failures
> with their wounded memories.
> Let them not defeat me now.
> I know I cannot run away
> else I'm pursued by demons
> who take up sticks to beat
> me on my road to Jericho.
> Neither can I hide in tombs
> of dark regrets, only looking out.
> So walk with me as I step
> out in the light, encountering
> who I am, as part of who I was
> and loving
> all the disaffected parts of me.

PRAYER: (Pray the Lord's Prayer.)
Especially this day, my delivering God, deliver me from evil.

DAY 35 COME HOME TO YOURSELF

READ: Luke 15: 11-24

> *" ... when he came to himself, he said, 'How many of my father's hired hands have bread enough and to spare, and here I am dying of hunger! I will get up and go to my father ...'" Luke 15:17-18*

The son, who wasted his inheritance, did not respect either himself or his resources. He had to hit bottom before he began to understand who he was. He repented and went to his Father, hoping to become a hired servant. Instead, he learned that his father was merciful and loving.

Discover who you really are to God.

We come home to ourselves as we discover who we are and what God is like.

WHERE IS HOME?

Where is home when I am young
and go away to school?
Where is home when I am small
and parents die or divorce?
Where is home, in middle years
when I am unemployed
or moving on to other spheres?
Where is home when I am old
and need some nursing care
or pull up roots to move
so my children can be there?

Verna G. Smith

> Home is the place within
> where I begin to love
> and understand myself
> where demons are released
> and God is present
> and I begin to see
> all of God's children
> differently.

PRAYER: My loving God, who calls me home to myself and to you. Thank you for receiving me, not as a hired servant, but as your true child.

DAY 36 SEEK OPPORTUNITIES IN DIMINISHMENTS

READ: 2 Corinthians 4:16-18

> *... we do not lose heart. Even though our outer nature is wasting away, our inner nature is being renewed day by day. ... 2 Corinthians 4:16*

Diminishments confront us all through life; but especially when we are aging.

In our diminishments God may have something to say to us. Opportunities to hear those messages often come when we least expect them. When our declining powers make us fearful or angry we need to take time to listen more carefully.

> If I'm loving and I really care
> Will I worry about diminishments?
> If I'm trusting and I'm feeling safe
> Will my diminishments trouble me?
>
> I have loved my expansions
> and my growing strength
> and what importance I have known
> Yes, to be important
> to some or to many.
> I don't want to be forgotten.
>
> But my diminishments prepare
> me for another life.
> I have some glimmers.

Verna G. Smith

>So the other life will bring
>surprises and expansions of its own.
>Since I am a little lower than
>the angels now
>what will I become?
>Can I trust the One
>who does not forget,
>who notices a sparrow's fall?
>
>What is God's call to you today?

PRAYER: Help me bless the lives of people with my words
Help me honor you with my thoughts that form the words.
Help me be attentive to your opportunities.

DAY 37 DISCOVER GOD'S PURPOSE FOR YOU.

READ: Philippians 3:12-16

I press on toward the goal for the prize of the heavenly call of God in Christ Jesus.
Philippians 3:14

Be **Present** to God
Receive God's **Power**
Find God's **Purpose**

Living without purpose
is like bobbing on a sea of doubt
with no means for navigation.

Is my purpose obvious
already given me
to nurture and protect
like a fragile garden plant

or elusive like the first
violet in spring
waiting my discovery?

"Wait upon the Lord.
Find God's purpose for your life.
Do your work, and be yourself."
—— Attributed to Phillips Brooks

PRAYER: My purposeful God
if I do not know my purpose
show it to me.

Verna G. Smith

If I knew it once
and it has changed
reveal it now.

Be merciful to me.

DAY 38 FIND WHERE YOU BELONG.

READ: I Corinthians 12:4-27

> *For just as the body is one and has many members, and all the members of the body, though many, are one body, so it is with Christ. ... If one member suffers, all suffer together with it; if one member is honored, all rejoice together with it.*
> *1 Corinthians 12:12, 26*

We all need to be a part of God's intimate family. Let God lead you into a small close-knit community where Christ is honored, and where trust enables you to be yourself and share your pilgrimage. There you can bear each other's burdens and share your joys. We need the love and help, and especially the prayers, of each other, in our Christian community.

As we grow close to each other we may be tempted to envy the gifts of others or take pride in our own. We do not need to compare ourselves to other people. Each of us has different gifts and all have the same God who values us as we are. Our diversity contributes to the strength of the body of Christ when we learn to work together toward God's purposes.

> *"You're blessed when you can show people how to cooperate instead of compete or fight. That's when you discover who you really are, and your place in God's family. ..."*
> *Matthew 5:9 THE MESSAGE*

A trusting community can encourage us to share our shortcomings as well as our strengths. *"Confess your sins to one another and pray for one another, so that you may be healed."* (James 5:16) Confession brings healing and release of energy. But we need to select with care, those who will hear the secrets of our heart. They help us maintain our integrity before God. Otherwise, our abilities to deceive ourselves are almost unlimited.

If you have not yet found a nurturing community, ask God to help you find it.

> Our community, a garden of hope
> opens its floral buds to God
> releases fragrance with its colors,
> pink of love
> red of courage
> white of purity
> yellow of enlightenment
> lavender of loyalty
> Our community of hope empowers the children of our God.

PRAYER: My valuing God, thank you that you give us community to help each other in living with you and serving you. Keep us in your care.

DAY 39 LIVE WITH EQUILIBRIUM

READ: John 6:1-15

> *When Jesus realized that they were about to come and take him by force to make him king, he withdrew again to the mountain by himself. John 6:15*

Jesus was reluctant to receive peoples' adulation. He knew how easy, and destructive, such basking in their glory could become. He understood that hero worship could distract him from his Father's purpose. After he feed the five thousand, people thronged about him to make him king. By withdrawing, he set his boundaries and protected himself.

> *The purity of silver and gold can be tested in a crucible, but a man (person) is tested by his reaction to people's praise. Proverbs 27:21 The Living Bible*

The desert monks, whose solitude helped develop expertise in living, taught, "Live with dispassion."[v] Dispassion is being objective about outcomes: not overwhelmed by bad news; not inflated by good. Dispassion does not mean indifference. We accept life, and all that it contains, with thanksgiving. We learn not to be overly attached to our possessions or to our blessings. And in our dispassion, we discover freedom.

> Fear hovers deep inside me like a bird of prey
> waiting to attack my vulnerability:
> increasing years; declining strength.
> Like a frightened mouse, I want to run away
> But, the bird's sharp eye will see me and
> subvert my panicky attempts to help myself.

Verna G. Smith

> I'll dismiss this bird to God
> who calls me now to inner work
> To go into a task with trust, knowing
> God will give me balance in success
> and in my failure, peace.

PRAYER: My valuing God, when I am praised, protect me from inflating myself. Help me pass through inflation's test more refined, like silver or gold from the furnace. When I am criticized, or when I fail, protect me from self-hate. Fill me with your trust. Give me a heart that is dispassionate, and not indifferent.

DAY 40 LIVE VICTORIOUSLY

READ: John 17:1-25

> *"... Holy Father, protect them in your name that you have given me, so that they may be one, as we are one. ... I speak these things in the world so that they may have my joy made complete in themselves. ... I am not asking you to take them out of the world, but I ask you to protect them from the evil one."*
> John 17:11, 13, 15

Daily, we are bombarded with bad news. If we don't experience it close at hand, we see it or read about it in the media. We know the suffering in our world. Because of such pain we may allow discouraging thoughts to defeat us. But our ultimate dependency is not upon the world, nor upon any person in the world. It is upon God.

> When we meditate upon God's cross
> a somber mood sometimes overwhelms
> We forget that death fulfills our lives
> and forms a prelude to eternity.
>
> Our cross of Christ protects us
> from the darkness that could overtake
> and destroy our lives with evil.
>
> Our cross of Christ reminds us
> how He came to give us life victoriously
> and teach us what our God is like.

Try this ancient (modified) prayer before going to sleep and upon awakening.

Verna G. Smith

        Almighty God
        Shine your light upon me
        Protect me with your cross
        Cover my sins with your life-blood
        Filter every influence through
        your love and wisdom
        Deliver me from evil.

PRAYER: Father God, you called me from death to life to live victoriously, transcending barriers that cut me off from you.

Save me from clinging to the past or fearing the future.
Lift me by your spirit. Have mercy upon me. Amen.

ABOUT THE AUTHOR

Verna G. Smith is the mother of four grown children, and served for five years as a missionary in the Philippines. She has given spiritual direction to individuals and groups, after earning a Certificate in Spiritual Direction at San Francisco Theological Seminary. As school psychologist, she was particularly helpful to teachers and parents with problem children. For several years she served as staff psychologist in a residential community for male juvenile offenders These meditations share insights from her rich spiritual journey, as she has struggled with painful childhood memories. She also is the author of "Apples of Gold," another book of meditations.

END NOTES

[i] Adapted from "Bread of the World in Mercy Broken," by Reginald Heber.

[ii] Martindale, Wayne, and Root, Jerry, editors, THE QUOTABLE LEWIS.
Tyndale House Publishers, 1989.

[iii] 3. Norris, Kathleen. DAKOTA. New York: Houghton Mifflin Company, 1993. p. 102.

[iv] Palmer, G.E.H. et. al. trans. eds. THE PHILOKALIA. London, Boston: Faber and Faber, 1984. vol I, p. 36

[v] THE PHILOKALIA. v.III, p. 357.

Breinigsville, PA USA
26 July 2010
242421BV00002B/25/A